The Library of
HOLIDAYS™

Groundhog Day

Amy Margaret

The Rosen Publishing Group's
PowerKids Press™
New York

For Allie and Ana

Published in 2002 by The Rosen Publishing Group, Inc.
29 East 21st Street, New York, NY 10010

First Edition

Book Design: Michael Caroleo and Michael de Guzman
Project Editors: Jennifer Landau, Jennifer Quasha, Joanne Randolph

Photo credits: pp. 4, 7 © Kennan Ward/ CORBIS; p. 8 © Hulton-Deutsch Collection/CORBIS; p. 11 © Lake County Museum/CORBIS; p. 12 © Reuters/Jason Cohn/Archive Photos; pp. 15, 19 © Reuters NewMedia Inc./CORBIS; p. 16 © Bettmann/CORBIS; p. 20 © The Everett Collection; p. 22 © Joe McDonald/CORBIS.

Margaret, Amy.
Groundhog day / by Amy Margaret.— 1st ed.
    p. cm. — (The library of holidays)
Includes bibliographical references and index.
  ISBN 0–8239–5785–3 (lib. bdg.)
1. Groundhog Day—Juvenile literature. [1. Groundhog Day. 2. Holidays.] I. Margaret, Amy. II. Title.
  GT4995.G76 M37 2002
  394.261-dc21

00–012984

Manufactured in the United States of America

Contents

It's Groundhog Day!

Every year on February 2, people throughout the United States get up early to find out whether a groundhog will see its shadow when it leaves its **burrow**. This holiday is called Groundhog Day. According to **tradition**, if a groundhog sees its shadow there will be six more weeks of winter. If a groundhog doesn't see its shadow, tradition has it that there will be an early spring and the groundhog will stay above ground.

◀ *If a groundhog sees its shadow, tradition says that there will be six more weeks of winter.*

The Groundhog

A groundhog is a small, furry **mammal**. It also is called a woodchuck. It lives in an underground burrow that it digs for itself. Most groundhogs live in Canada and the eastern United States. A groundhog **hibernates** during the winter. A groundhog is an **herbivore**, or plant eater. It has sharp claws and pointed teeth. An adult groundhog is about 15 inches (38 cm) long with a 6-inch (15.2-cm) tail.

Groundhogs eat seeds, roots, and grasses. ▶

The Origins of Groundhog Day

Before there was Groundhog Day, February 2 held another meaning. Starting around A.D. 350, **Christians** called the day Candlemas. On Candlemas Day, Christians remember Mary and Joseph's first visit to the temple with the infant Jesus. It is called Candlemas because many carried candles to honor Jesus' mother, Mary. In Germany, people believed that on Candlemas Day a hedgehog could **predict** how long winter would last.

◀ *Candlemas Day is still celebrated today. This woman is praying to honor the day.*

Punxsutawney, Pennsylvania

Punxsutawney, Pennsylvania, is where Groundhog Day started in North America. In the mid-1700s, Native Americans called the area Ponksaduteney, which means "town of the sandflies." Over the years Ponksaduteney became "Punxsutawney." In the late 1790s, German settlers brought the tradition of Candlemas to Punxsutawney. They believed a hedgehog could predict the weather. There were no hedgehogs in the area, so they **adopted** the groundhog for the tradition.

This is a postcard from Punxsutawney, Pennsylvania. ▶

The Birth of Groundhog Day

On February 2, 1886, people in Punxsutawney gathered to watch a groundhog peek out of its hole. He was named Punxsutawney Phil. The local newspaper carried an article about the groundhog that did not see its shadow. This was the first official record of Groundhog Day in Punxsutawney. The next year Gobbler's Knob became the official site for the groundhog's **festivities**. Gobbler's Knob is a wooded area on a small hill outside Punxsutawney.

Punxsutawney Phil, shown in this picture, makes his Groundhog Day appearance.

Since the 1800s, Punxsutawney Phil's name has been passed down to each groundhog that inherits his job. Today Phil lives in Punxsutawney in the Groundhog Zoo. The zoo was built in the mid-1970s. Phil, his **mate** Phyllis, his cousin Barney, and a few other groundhogs share the home. Phil spends most of his time sleeping and wandering around the zoo, except on February 2, Groundhog Day!

Punxsutawney Phil spends most days sleeping and eating. On Groundhog Day, however, ▶ he is the center of attention.

Punxsutawney Phil's Predictions

Phil has been predicting the weather since 1887. Of the times he has popped out of his hole to date, Phil has seen his shadow 90 times and has not seen it 14 times. There is no record for nine of the years. During this time period, Phil has predicted the weather correctly only 39 percent of the time. Even though he has a fairly low **accuracy** rate, the popularity of Phil's predictions continue. They are front-page news in many English-speaking countries around the world.

◀ *In this photograph from 1985, Phil has just seen his shadow. That means six more weeks of winter!*

Other Groundhogs

Many states have their own groundhog to watch on Groundhog Day. The people of Sun Prairie, Wisconsin, believe that their town is the Groundhog Capital of the World. They watch for their local groundhog, Jimmy, to appear each February. Canada also has a few weather-forecasting groundhogs. The most famous one was Wiarton Willie. He was an **albino** groundhog. From 1956 to 1999, Wiarton Willie had a 90 percent accuracy rate on his forecasts.

Wiarton Willie, shown here, was Canada's most famous groundhog. ▶

Punxsutawney Today

A 1993 movie called *Groundhog Day* is set in Punxsutawney, although it was not filmed there. The people who made the movie used some of the same store names as those in Punxsutawney, though. They even used the groundhog-head garbage cans and official Groundhog Day flags that line the small town's streets. Since the movie, more than 30,000 people have traveled to Punxsutawney, Pennsylvania, each February to see Phil, Punxsutawney's own groundhog.

◀ This is a scene from Groundhog Day, *with actor Bill Murray standing in front of a set made to look like Gobbler's Knob in Punxsutawney.*

Celebrate Groundhog Day

There are many ways that you can celebrate Groundhog Day. If you live near a place that has its own groundhog, you can watch the event in person. You also can watch for the groundhog's shadow on television. After the groundhog's prediction, look outside and make your own weather prediction. You also can watch the movie *Groundhog Day*. However you celebrate, remember that this holiday is an important part of America's history.

Glossary

accuracy (A-kyuh-ruh-see) How close something is to being correct.

adopted (uh-DOP-ted) To have taken on someone else's beliefs.

albino (al-BY-noh) A mammal lacking color in its skin and eyes. Albinos usually have white skin or fur and pink or red eyes.

burrow (BUR-oh) A hole an animal digs in the ground for shelter.

Christians (KRIS-chunz) People who follow the teachings of Jesus Christ and the Bible.

festivities (fes-TIH-vih-teez) Large parties or gatherings.

herbivore (ER-bih-vor) One who eats only plants.

hibernates (HY-bur-nayts) Spends the winter sleeping or resting.

mammal (MAM-uhl) A kind of animal that is warm-blooded and has a backbone.

mate (MAYT) The male or female of a pair of animals.

predict (pre-DIKT) To make a guess based on facts or information.

tradition (truh-DIH-shun) A way of doing something that is passed down.

Index

Web Sites

To learn more about Groundhog Day, check out this Web site:
www.groundhogsday.com

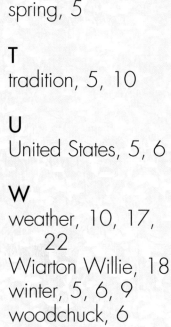